For more information contact:
Pleasurable Pause Press, LLC
1730 White Avenue
Beloit, Wisconsin 53511
www.pleasurablepausepress.com

FIRST EDITION

Design:
Jeff Larson
Larson Design Company

Typography:
Titles: Montana, Body: Minion Pro, Subtitles: Madelyn,
Journals: Noteworthy, Sketches: Janda Everyday Casual

Printer:
Lifetouch Production / Rockford Litho Center

Library of Congress Cataloging-in-Publication Data is available upon request.

ISBN 978-0-9816499-2-4

Photographic Credits

Cover:
Jeanne Sturges Holbrook

Interior:
Maisie Lewis, Jeff Larson, Ryan Stanyard, Lea Spicer, Anne Goodwin,
Matthew Goodwin, Benjamin Goodwin, Lynn Wood, Mary Widder, PL 64, Dani Hill.

Illustration Page 60:
Gerle Shagdar

Back Cover:
Jeanne Sturges Holbrook

Author Photo:
Fred Leonard

COME TO THE LAKE

This book is dedicated to Kathryn Goodwin,
aka Kayo, Spirit Keeper on Pleasant Lake.

SKIPPING STONES

It's a beautiful summer day at the world's most pleasant place. The canoe has brought us to this spot. We search the water for stones, each with a different purpose in mind. Hers, to find yet another rock unique and beautiful enough to add to her collection; mine, to find the thinnest, flattest, most perfect skipper. After several valiant attempts at "launching one" across the lake, I stumble upon the perfect stone. With pride and excitement, I show Grandma Kayo the stone that will make me a famous skipper, and before I let it fly, she points out that what I hold is actually an arrowhead. Needless to say, I lost the urge to skip that particular stone, and it was the beginning of my rock collecting days.

Son Tom's eulogy to Grandma Kayo

PLEASANT LAKE GIRL

I became a Pleasant Lake girl thirty-five years ago.
The rite of passage is simple: One must simply, truly love life at
The Lake. That means swimming across it, searching for sunbeams
as you glide under its fresh water surface and charting long hours
in sailboats, canoes and kayaks. It also requires being immersed in
the rhythm of the Lake, which means opening books instead
of pushing buttons, and always being available for a round of
backgammon, chess or multi-level card house construction.
A Pleasant Lake girl knows how to build a crackling fire and can
spend hours in the back bays investigating turtledoms and
Heron nests as the sun blazes across the sky. For the many who
have graced these shores before us, we remain their spirit keepers
in our fresh water paradise and continue to celebrate the
discoveries of Pleasant Lake girls.

COME TO THE LAKE

Reflections on a Cottage Life

Anne Goodwin

REFLECTIONS

THE COTTAGES

THE FUTURE

I grew up preparing to be a Pleasant Lake Girl without knowing it. I happily attended as many weeks of Wisconsin YMCA camp that my parents would spring for. My being the youngest of five siblings, they sponsored several, enjoying the break in home life routine as much as I did. I decorated my personal canoe paddle, learned how to find dry firewood in the midst of pouring rain (find the lowest branches on an evergreen in the thick of the woods... guaranteed to snap crisp every time), and paddled endless hours through the mazes of fresh water lakes with four of my cabin mates and two counselors. We took on life large as we hit the trail. My core self formed during those summer weeks of exploration of both nature and relationships. Today, with the stroke of a canoe or kayak paddle I go straight to center and feel wonderfully at home.

My introduction to Pleasant Lake came unexpectedly from a first attempt at a casual fling, following several, multi-year 'serious relationships'. My fling came in the form of Matthew, a guitarist/songwriter who was divorced with two children, a traveling rock and roller, and a tad bit older than my naïve twenty-three years.

Definitely fling status, not relationship potential. On our third date
Matthew took me on a road trip to a place called Pleasant Lake, and
more specifically to his family cottage, fittingly named The Shelter.
The minute I walked down the hill, saw the glimmer of the lake,
inhaled the sweet, pungent 'old cottage' smell, and glimpsed the
vintage Old Town canoe on the rack I was struck by a surprising
sense of familiarity. Once we paddled out to the middle of the
pristine, no-wake lake (unheard of in these days of
Jet Skis, and Wave Runners) I knew my fling idea was backfiring
and I REALLY liked the guy. Ecstatic, I described my day of
connection with my mother. Aware of Matthew's seemingly
questionable personal resume, she cautioned me: "That's fine Anne.
Just don't let It (the lake plus Matthew) affect your Future."
(Update… thirty years ago, Matthew became her darling son-in-law
and I, proudly, an official Pleasant Lake girl.)

THE SHELTER

Kathryn, my mother in-law and dear friend, aka Kayo, was the original Pleasant Lake girl. She forged the path in full Lake Living. A grown woman with five young children, she led the way the summer they purchased the 1920s one-room cottage with boy and girl sleeping coveys, for a sizeable eight-thousand dollar chunk of hard-earned 1950s cash. She packed the station wagon the day school let out and checked her brood into the new (old) family cottage, christened The Shelter, by the name etched on the worn ring buoy hanging above the wooden door frame. The station wagon disappeared back into town with her husband, Gerry, for the work week and life at the Lake began in earnest. For Kathryn, that meant ritual swims across the lake, quick sails in the tricky, small-lake wind puffs (always a child or two in tow to absorb a basic lake-life skill), paddles in the Old Town canoe and Projects. Projects included re-canvassing the 1940's wooden canoe,

collecting field stones of interest in order to build a corner fireplace
and continually nurturing a blend of wild flowers and lovingly
tended transplants to fortify the lake's first 'naturalist approach' to
shoreline maintenance. Not for Kayo the 1950s concrete and
ruffled tin retaining walls that are now forever banned from
choking a Wisconsin lake shoreline. While other women baked
and cleaned and found sun solace on their piers, Kathryn would
busy herself building a brick walkway or refinishing a treasured
artifact to add to her collection of lake lore objects that slowly filled
The Shelter as the years swam by.

THE COTTAGE NEXT DOOR

We almost lost The Cottage Next Door to a crook and a thief.

Fortunately, in this case the bad guy did ultimately finish last.

Or at least without a stolen cottage.

When Kathryn and Gerry bought The Shelter, they eased some

of their property to Kathryn's brother Johnny, who hand-built a

tri-level rental cottage overlooking the lake. The path between

the two cottages was well worn by decades of cousins and family

friends shuttling back and forth during annual lake visits.

Enter the thief. In Johnny's later years, he became infirm and was

prey to Joe, an embezzler who specialized in stealing from the

elderly. Hell of a guy. He stole the Cottage Next Door by

'purchasing' it with Johnny's own money and made it a party palace

for all his criminal abettors. Kathryn, heartbroken, communicated

her displeasure and dismay by placing an old wooden sawhorse

between the cottages. The path was a path no more. Fortunately,

Matthew's cousin Lee, who lived in California, got wind something

was horribly awry with his father and spent a year in Wisconsin

with Johnny, reclaiming what he could of his dad's estate.

The Cottage Next Door was one of those assets.

Cousin Lee and his siblings eventually sold The Cottage Next Door to my brother Rob and me. It was in horrific shape; others would have started fixing it up by tearing it down.

Fortunately we are cottage people and set about to reclaim it…one square inch at a time. Our thought was to prepare it for rental but once we brought it back to its original charm and added some of our own, I moved right in.

So now, Matthew and I are not only husband and wife, but lake neighbors as well. The path between the two cottages is once again open for the next generation of cousins and grandchildren to tramp along. And the guy next door uses it quite often as well.

HILLTOP

Interestingly, the story of Hilltop also has a bad guy, conflict and happy ending. This is a classic tale about a Cinderella shack: Back in the 1980s, a nebulous developer surreptitiously purchased the Boy Scout Camp across the lake masking his true intentions for the land. He planned to erect on-site more than 200 perched modular 'mill' homes, each featuring two bedrooms, one bath and a living area all contained within 700 sq. feet. The density impact with his plan would have devastated the health of Pleasant Lake, thus the birth of the Pleasant Lake Association.

Ten years in the court system and the PLA prevailed.

The guy disappeared in the night and left a model of his 'cabin' behind. Enter Matthew's Uncle Johnny. Ever the resourceful 'collector', he claimed the model structure, hauled it across the frozen lake and plopped it on some cement blocks, top of the hill behind his cottage. He filled it with 'treasures' for the next twenty years. Legend on the lake was if you couldn't find what you were looking for at Ace hardware, chances were you'd find it in Johnny's Shed. Looking for a miter saw? He probably had four of them. When Johnny became infirm and moved from his cottage, the Shed remained full to the brim and closed up for years.

It took a crew of three men four days to empty the Shack turned

Shed once my brother and I bought The Cottage Next Door and its iffy outbuilding. I hired the crew immediately after finding a cozy, nesting family of mice in the first dank file drawer I opened. After the 'treasures' were hauled away, we spent the next twelve years using the structure for boat, grill, and lawn accessory storage. All the while dancing around the idea of someday making the space functional. That's what we did. And something really special happened. The birth of Hilltop involved replacing every surface, freshly painting everything from tip to toe and adding a screen porch with a lake view! The hilltop where Johnny planted his new

shed proved to be a spectacular site with an incredible ethos. We like to think the Pottawatomie, who used the shores of Pleasant Lake to sharpen tools, fish, and cook, made camp on this hill overlooking the lake. Hilltop reflects a great sense of spirit and quiet. A perfect place to experience a pleasurable pause.

BOYVILLE

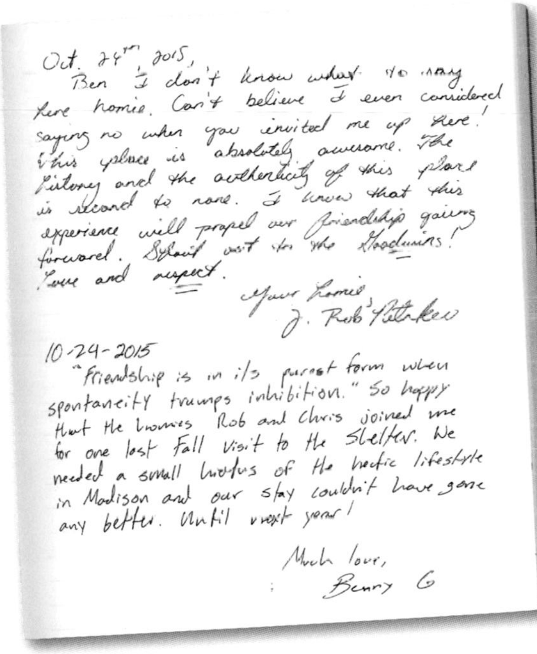

Oct. 24th, 2015,

Ben, I don't know what to say here homie. Can't believe I even considered saying no when you invited me up here! This place is absolutely awesome. The history and the authenticity of this place is second to none. I know that this experience will propel our friendship going forward. Shout out to the Goodwins! Love and respect.

Your homie,
J. Rob Petrikev

10-24-2015

"Friendship is in its purest form when spontaneity trumps inhibition." So happy that the homies Rob and Chris joined me for one last Fall visit to the Shelter. We needed a small hiatus of the hectic lifestyle in Madison and our stay couldn't have gone any better. Until next year!

Much love,
Benny G

Formula to success in captivating two young boys in a device-free summer of cottage lake life: increase the number of boys from two to six.

the best part was swimming
across the lake we also
went canoeing. Kyaking.
I can't wait to come back.

— Eric 8-21-02

I began a forty-two minute Mom shuttle from our
hometown to Pleasant Lake that began the minute school let out
and continued until the last moments of summer dripped away.
Drop off two, pick up two and keep a couple extra on hand
at all times.

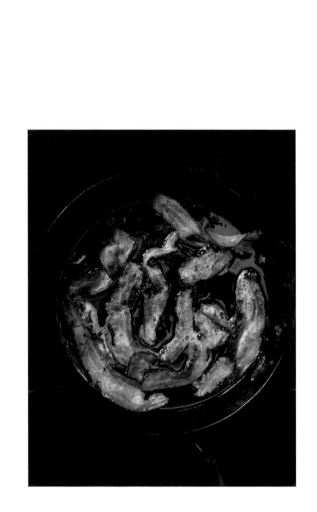

The secret to waking a cottage full of sleeping boys? Start sizzling pounds of thick-slabbed bacon in the cast iron skillet and wait. Usually by the time I deep-fried the last bit of stale French or Italian bread in the copious amount of bacon grease for my beyond-decadent French toast, sleepy heads would emerge and congregate around the table outside on the deck.

And then the day would begin. First visits always began with the obligatory pier-to-pier swim test to ensure water safety and to provide each boy with a challenge and usually the path to accomplishment. "Yes! I passed! And now I'm a raft swimmer!" became the lake mantra most heard on our pier.

Made-up games were endless…King Of The Raft,

Chittering (spitting contest of cherry pits from deck to lake),

Run!Jump!Dive!, Under-Water Talking and any kind of

throwing and catching activity went on all day.

If by chance there was a lull, I produced a three page By Lake and

By Land scavenger hunt and launched them in various water craft

to discover the Lake's treasures. 500 points awarded for a Native

American arrowhead kept them engaged for hours. A rare few

have been extracted from our shores.

Searching for Rocks-With-Holes is a favorite activity (starting

with Kayo) and each cottage displays an Add-A-Rock

rope celebrating these unique finds.

 Old-fashioned board games filled the hours as well. Languid afternoons found carefully guarded, stacked piles of Monopoly money or the whir of the 'Game of Life' in the air as hours passed by with the boys determined not to succumb to the designated pratfalls and to come out 'on top'.

Girls had their place in Boyville as well. At first, as youngsters, the boys were all about 'raiding' the Girl Scout camp just down the lakeshore. Rob and Ben tried to re-enact their older brothers' escapades but fell a wee bit short in their efforts.

After hours of carefully staging a night-time stealth attack which included leaving their boxer shorts on the Girl Scouts' pier and me nixing Hershey's chocolate sauce added to the mix, the plan culminated with a plea, "Mom, can you paddle over there with us, in case we get caught?" No, Girl Scout camp raids of yore did not include parental accompaniment. I am thankful we did not receive any late night phone calls.

"Ring the bell and run like hell,"
Gus

The next phase of girls were real live peers on a neighbor's pier with an endless array of changing bikinis. That's when King of The Raft took on a whole new level of intensity and when new lifelong friendships were forged. And the games continued. New to our guys, and much to their amazement and probably chagrin, they became quite good at Charades. And any other game the girls deemed worthy playing. As bodies matured and interests were sparked, dreams of summer romances percolated around us. Although those never took flame, the friendships of the boys and girls of summer forever hold steadfast and true.

Now they are all grown up. Occasionally we are blessed with their return and they find not much has changed at Pleasant Lake. Although the new raft barely supports the accumulated weight of adult warriors as they continue the quest of King, we all shift back into the routines of that special time, play the old games and ease back into cottage living. What's that smell? Oh, just the bacon frying. Time's awastin', boys.

Cody Shober's comment tucking into the
cottage next door in the threat of an
impending thunderstorm: "maybe we should
move to "The Shelter"!!

7 June 04

SIX BOYS.
A SUMMER STORM.
THE SHELTER AND
THE COTTAGE NEXT DOOR.

'Our dry towel pile is soaked. After numerous jumping jacks our steel-poled table umbrella is snapped. Our upstairs is a camping trip gone awry. Gaping backpacks, duffel bags, assorted clothes, hidden forbidden electronics, all sit in an interior lake under the open windows. Wet 'everything' in a row.' (Anne's journal entry.)

Six boys gathered together for a weekend visit to the lake. Dutifully they brought all their belongings to the upstairs sleeping loft before quickly changing into their swim suits to pounce on every available lake toy. Kayaks, canoes, paddle boats, all hit the lake simultaneously and their boisterous antics began. And then a little breeze appeared. Within minutes an ominous dark green sky began forming in the west. The breeze immediately turned into gusts and I shouted to the boys to quickly batten down the waterfront.

All craft and boys needed to be out of the water pronto. Driving, slanted rain pelted us as we secured the lakefront. We were all impressed with our ability to react so quickly to Mother Nature's surprise attack.

Then we looked up the hill at the cottages. That's when we witnessed the table umbrella doing its calisthenics. And saw that every lake-facing window and door was wide open to the gale force pounding us. That was the moment the Boyville Brigade and I learned to always separate forces during the approach of a summer storm. Later, wrapped in blankets in front of a crackling fire, we all realized that clothes, electronics, sleeping bags, and pillows are all optional to making a Pleasant Lake visit great.

PLEASANT LAKE

SCAVENGER HUNT

LAKE LIST

(points)

10	Bass-striped fish
15	Turtle on Log
10	Extra on Log (each)
15	Green Heron
15	Connected Dragon Flies
20	Turtle Under Water
10	Clam
20	Great Blue Heron
30	Box Under Water With Rocks
10	Buddy Board (each)
20	Willow in Lake
30	Building Permit on Tree
20	Black Bird with Orange Wing
10	Chasing Brown Bird
15	Port-a-Potty
15	Purple Row Boat
15	Fish Spawning Bed (each)

LAND LIST

(points)

15	Caterpillar
15	Mulberry Tree
10	Turtle (Wooden)
15	Bird House (each)
25	Poison Ivy
25	Thermometer
30	Sea Gull Statue
50	Toad/Frog
50	Deer

Come Back With

150	Rock With Hole
500	Arrow Head
25	Sand From Beach
50	# of Piers on Lake
30	# of Boat Houses
75	# of Buoys

To Collect

20	20 pieces of Kindling
30	10 Medium Logs
30	3 Big Logs

12 June 2003

Memories are being made at this moment... Bobby and the "sleepover bunch" are planning, plotting, scouting and exact executing their very first Girl Scout Camp Raid. "Captain Underpants" is going to leave a boys' "size 12 specimen" with a note attached. warning of further visits. Much thought and discussion has gone into this mission — I hope it

sleepover bunch - like Rockwell, Jason Mal... Mitch and ...

We'll be back.

FAMILY, FRIENDS, FOOD
& FRESH WATER FUN

"I had the best day ever"

August

Life changes at the Lake. Especially for that wondrous,
ever-evolving small group known as 'family'. The Shelter has
provided lake therapy for many families for generations.
The Cottage Next Door as well.

I always breathe a sigh of relief once we walk down the hill returning
to life at the Lake. Our insistence (especially in the early years) that
the cottages be electronic device-free zones requires all of us to
'family' differently. We share small space. We talk to each other.
We play together be it on shore or off. Board games (Scrabble or
Chess anyone?), endless hands of Euchre and all forms of water
activity means we are choosing to engage. Lake life constantly weaves
new texture, fiber and color into the fabric of our family

We are on our third generation of raising children at Pleasant Lake.

The raft has been rebuilt countless times as have the piers.

We've gone from a single canoe and row boat family to a waterfront now filled with kayaks, additional canoes, stand-up paddle boards and a trusty old toddler-friendly paddle boat. Our motto for that particular craft is 'how to get nowhere fast'. However, it does make a useful beverage and buffet boat during Girls' Night! Happily, we have yet to succumb to any craft that requires a motor.

Our grandchildren swim the same swim test and follow the same lake rules established early on by Grandma Kayo. The rhythm of Pleasant Lake life has not skipped a beat as our family expands.

One of the best parts of family life at Pleasant Lake is the number of other families who have shared our lake traditions.

Matthew's parents generously vacated the Shelter (not an easy sacrifice considering the short length of Wisconsin summers) so others could enjoy extended lake visits. Matthew and his brother Roger have continued that generosity.

The Burke family just celebrated their 37th year choosing Pleasant Lake as a destination location for their yearly multi-generational summer vacation. Adult cousins from Florida and California with various spouses and offspring also count on their annual pilgrimage to Pleasant Lake. Friends, who we consider family, check-in regularly and bask in returning to our well known rituals.

One of our favorite group activities is convening at sunset in the middle of the lake in a makeshift flotilla to enjoy our 360-degree view as the day dims around us. It's usually at this point when we are constantly amazed how this postage-stamp of a lake and these postage-stamp size cottages continue to make such a mighty ripple in so many lives.

SWAMP BOY

My son Rob once informed us when we picked him up from
a YMCA summer camp renowned for its outdoor adventure
programs, "You know, I am not really that fond of Nature".
And I believe I know the moment in his life when he had this
revelation. In some ways, I can't blame him. The day he decided
Nature wasn't his friend is also the day I declared him my hero.
For several years, the Larson family checked into the Shelter as
our guests. The first year, Robby, age twelve, met Allie, age eleven,
he offered to show the Larsons the lake. All seventy-two pounds
of him insisted on commanding Matthew's granddaddy kayak
as he led an entourage of canoes, kayaks and a paddle boat off
on their great explore. Imagine my surprise when the contingency
all returned minus one large green kayak and one fearless leader.
I could not get in my kayak fast enough when I heard the reason why.

We have a 'nursery' at the lake....an inner sanctum bay that one accesses by going through the 'Secret Passage'. It's where the Sandhill Cranes, Great Blue Herons, assorted turtles and hundreds of other species of fauna and wildlife congregate to raise their young, feed, and

find sanctuary. By the time August arrives, it becomes almost jungle-like, teeming with percolating boggy clumps and thick-as-carpet water lilies. Paddling through the dense pads and tunnels of towering cattails and marsh grasses reminds me of some far eastern rice paddy—definitely 'other worldly'.

It was August when the Larsons arrived. When Rob, in his bravado offered to escort the group through the Secret Passage, they assessed the situation, determined the boggy path impassable and turned

back. My tenacious twelve year-old, determined to impress a certain little someone, sallied forth into the swamp. "He's where? And you left him?" I asked with my voice rising as I scrambled into my kayak and took off for the Back Bay.

Half-way there, in the middle of the lake, I see a small bobbing head swimming towards me. And discover a very humbled Robby making his way home. "Where's Dad's kayak?" I ask, not really relishing the answer. "In the middle of the swamp". Robby's fierceness drove him into the middle of the bog, but his slight stature and fatigue did not allow him to paddle out. "So", he explained to me, "I folded my clothes and left them on the kayak so you would know that I had left the boat on purpose if you came looking for me and found it empty." Which meant he entered a bottomless murk of spongy, pungent, mucky water that at the highest point came up to his neck, with all sorts of slimy, creepy swamp paraphernalia attaching to him as he made his way through. "You know, we have to go fetch the kayak", I informed him, so he draped himself over my bow and we headed to the entrance of the Secret Passage. And then we stopped. I could not paddle through the floating carpet of muck to where Matthew's kayak waited, cradled in the gurgling bosom of the bog. That's when my boy became a man in front of my eyes, "I'll go get it Mom, I left it", and dang if he didn't re-enter the quagmire, trudge through chest deep yuck and return with kayak towed in hand. If only Allie could have witnessed that feat! That's when he became my hero and he decided, down to his bones perhaps, that he really wasn't that fond of Nature.

PURPLE GOLD

Kayo's family enjoyed the pursuit and the bounty of Wisconsin's
wild grape starting in the mid-1800's. She faithfully followed her
grandfather's coveted grape jelly making every September. Often
her supply came from a precious vine growing along a fence line on
Pleasant Lake Road. She not only shared her spirit legacy of life on
Pleasant Lake with me, she also passed on her jelly-making
tradition. It's an honor I carry with pleasure. Except those grapes
are not easy to come by. Some years vines produce, some years not.
I have a theory…when the August weeds are high and dense in the
lake, the grapes will be plentiful on the vine. Or is it when they are
low and sparse? Never quite sure. It usually takes a buddy to go
grape fishing, one to keep an eye on the country road, and
the other to hang out the car window with an eagle eye for the
well-camouflaged grape.

Wild grapes are just a smidge bigger than a currant.

So one needs a lot of them to make a vat of grape jelly. We now
call it our Purple Gold, it is a precious commodity. I give it away
as hostess gifts only after the recipient passes a grilling on whether
they really, really like the idea of it. And then after their first taste,
they are thrilled to have it. The unique intensity, brightness, and
tartness of the wild grape makes Welches' standard appear to be
congealed grape Kool-Aid.

The wild flavor alone makes all the work well worth it. The joyful recognition on Matthew's face, as he revisits his childhood, inhaling the familiar simmering aroma wafting through the house is priceless to me. The real joy is now the next generation entering the cottage, greeting me first with, "Do you have jelly, Grandma Anne?" and then a proper hello. Granddaughter Lucy and her first cousin/bestie/and almost sister Abby, go straight to the red stool in the kitchen and start pulling out the Pepperidge Farm Very Thin white bread to get the toast started. I think it is soon time to share the location of the vine with them. I am sure that Kathryn is smiling upon their happy, purple smiles from above.

WILD GRAPE JELLY

Pick grocery bags full of wild grape clusters. Do not worry about separating the grape from the stem. Use big old jelly-making pot (usually found in thrift/antique stores), add about an inch of water and gently simmer grape clusters, occasionally smashing them until all grapes are crushed. I usually lightly tent with aluminum foil while simmering. Strain grape liquid while crushing even more juice out of the grape remnants using a jelly sieve and pestle. Follow jelly-making instructions on Sure Gel package. I invert my hot-filled jelly jars once poured and after five minutes return to standing for a tight seal. When you hear the lids 'pop' and see the indent you have a safe seal. Store in dark cool space.

"What a nice thing to have...a place to come to."

←♡⊰

NOTES FROM OUR GUESTS

Surprise—It's not raining! Travis and I out after dinner for a canoe paddle, "I love these!" cherries, and now some major card games. I expect the whiskey will flow freely, the cabin will fill with cigar smoke, and fortunes will be made and lost way into the wee hours...or I'll be asleep in an hour as the lake works its magic.

Lynn and Travis

Today Robby, Ben and I went out to swim and jump on the trampoline in the water. We did flips and jumps. But when we had to leave we just got done fishing!! What fun!!

Ryan (belongs to Lynn and Travis)

Thanks so much Goodwins for our brief stay, here at P-Lake. We were glad to be able to spend some time at a place that was so important to my Dad. P-Lake is as beautiful and replenishing as ever. Truly a sacred place.

Love the Hinkleys (Matthew's cousins)

A Mother's Moment—Roscoe and Josh swam across the lake, together for the first time ever! (Roger too, but I'm not his mom). With Roscoe swimming toward the cottage and Josh toward the Blue Boathouse, they crossed mid-lake. Tears in my eyes, smile on my face and hands flying up in the air in amazement and jubilation. It's been a great day for us.

Susan, Roger, Roscoe, Josh (Matthew's brother and partner in The Shelter)

Today was one of the first true days of summer. It was wonderful to feel the glory of the sunshine! I accompanied Anne and Susan in the paddleboat as we followed Robby swimming in the cold lake to the grey raft. Jen and Todd were here and Jen and I fell asleep on the pier in the sun. These are the days we will always look back on with joy....all of us together at the lake.

Cassie (belongs to Roger, et al.)

Another beautiful PL experience. This one so different from the others. A whole new perspective. Cooler weather and first gray day led to experiencing fires in the Shelter. Wonderful warm glow and scents. Reading with my kids. Enjoying the cool breeze off the lake. And personally this was the most meaningful. I needed a few days of soul searching and reflection. Thank you to the soul, spirit and peace this heavenly treasure provides. And listening to Connor and Benny form such a wonderful friendship. Anne and Matt, you are wonderful friends, parents, and 'sharers of the lake'. Looking forward to more great memories. Thank you to the soul of the lake.

Jeff

Another great year at Pleasant Lake. Searching for anchors in fifteen feet of water and muck. Can't wait until next year!

Connor (belongs to Jeff)

Another awesome time at Pleasant Lake. Great weather, fun, and most of all, relaxation! Always so happy to be back and sad to leave, until next year that is. Can't wait—thanks for having us!

Allie (belongs to Connor and Jeff)

Thanks for letting us make ourselves at home. The canoe lesson was very memorable (wink). Let's do it again soon!

Becky and Kevin

JOURNAL ENTRY - *"Kevin left us riding the blaze of a harvest moon. Our hearts hurt and we miss him. Finding solace at the lake once again. Let the healing begin. Anne*

Hilltop—peaceful, birds all around. A sanctuary. To be here is so very special. A gift. Always a gift. Memories being made.

Becky

It's such a wonderful feeling being out at Pleasant Lake. It brings back old memories…and starts new ones all at the same time. So happy to be a part of the lake.

Meg (belongs to Becky and Kevin)

Life has so many blessings and for me this place, Pleasant Lake, is one of them. The true blessing is the love that flows from the waters...the refreshing spirit and the constant echo of laughter will haunt this ground through the ages! The two folks who have been a pillar of that love are Anne and Matthew, for without them this place would not reveal such goodness and hope. We must not forget the two angels who also roam here...Ben and The Robster. Those smiles can keep the world turning. Thanks for all the memories and allowing us to visit a little slice of Heaven on earth.

Little Tommy and Jeanne

So happy to arrive. Not so happy to leave. At least we had some fun in between!

Jeanne

We waited all year for this...its Pleasant Lake time! Celebrated with enthusiasm. It's official...the pier is in and the Season of the Sun has begun. We are thrilled to be back and to have been here to welcome it.

Dick and Dawn

Dear Friends...We'll remember this as the year the garbage truck ate the blue recycle bin. Trying to find a duplicate but no luck!

Beautiful 9 days of escape—hot days, cool nights. Both kids and grandkids came down and got wet and left happy. Kerry said 'when I'm here it's hard to believe there's a world where people are off to work, trying to make it through another day. This is Never-Neverland for us."

We loved it all...the rain, the thunder, the lightning, the sun, the wind, the water and the sky. Swam four times a day and read three books. A friend of Amy's said to us, "What a nice thing to have...a place to come to"

Thank you again, a hundred times over for this place to come to.

Always, Denny, Kathy, Amy and Kerry (37 years of annual lake visits)

Jason and I were married a little less than two months ago and our most exciting wedding gift was an overnight at the lake. This was even more special because I missed the Burke family visit—my first summer in 25 years without a dive off the pier. Until today. The sights and smells are the same comforting sensations of my youth, it is a blessing to have this place welcome us back each summer.

Kerry.

⇨—♡→

Goodwin tribe notes:

Robby, Anne and Uncle Robby swam across the lake today—a mirror lake.
Perfect for a long swim. Ben found an arrowhead next door on the
shoreline!

Anne

Incredible two days at the lake. The first, storm filled—winds blew the canoe
off the supports and moved the sailboat and anchor to shore. A cozy dinner
reaffirmed the name The Shelter. Today, bright blue sky, gentle wind, cool air
and the best skipperdippin' of the season. Bye PL.

Anne

My God what a summer! Our pier is out. The boys helped. The raft is out. But
not until seven beautiful teenagers played King of the Grope one more time.
Norman Rockwell died too soon. He would have painted Rob, Ben, Audrey,
Emily, Gus, Eric and Lexa closing the door on summer. Saturday night, all the
kids on the Big Bed playing Life. My dearest Anne fed the troops over, and
over, and over with love and tacos. She is now the 'heart' of Pleasant Lake. We
all revolve around her...Kayo is proud. Brothers, sister and cousins all visited
this summer. The love of family survives. Thank you Mom and Dad.

Matthew

The first visit of the year was fun. Climbing on the tree was fun.
We played the game Lava. I also made a village out of sticks.
I hope I come back next weekend.

Ben

Stellar summer at the lake. We've been in 'boyville' the whole time. Today Anne
and fellow Pleasant Lake girl, Lea, swam around the lake in honor of Kayo and
Marion Behrens who did the same feat annually into their 70's! We have much
to aspire to.

Anne

And we are off! After the usual major 'check-in ready for the season' overhaul, the season has officially begun. We had a special meeting of the Bonehead Club (Matthew, plus all four sons and new inductee grandson Sammy!) and a family work day. The Uncles all engaged in soccer, chess and wry banter with Sammy while Lucy and Grandma Anne had a most excellent kayak adventure. Windy lakedid not intimidate Miss Lucy Lu, she navigated through high seas, low bog, reedy reeds and 'grew in stature and grace' all along the way. All 42 pounds of her. Cousin Lee is 'back to the lake' as well as Roger and Susan...loving all the family time shared. Let's set the repeat button!

Anne

We did it...our annual swim around the lake! Me and Lea. Our summer checklist is now complete. Beautiful day for a swim. Too bad it is a Wednesday morning because we would be toasting ourselves right now instead of heading back to our workaday worlds.

Anne

Keepers of the cottages, where else in today's tumult can people of all ages, spend an hour together sharing dinner with a large, ancient turtle making his/her (hard to tell) way through fish remnants? The turtle was not hurried so why should we be?

Uncle Tom

Have been away too long. Am totally charmed by Hilltop especially the screened in porch. Thank you for sharing your beautiful PL and your generous hospitality. Love and more love!

Kathy and Rich

Seven turtles does not a red fox make!

'Yuncle Robby and Ben

We return to the lake like migrating birds. According to the customs of the golden earth.

Gerle and Rob

KAYO'S JOURNAL NOTES

Monday — June 1 – 1981
The first official day of my retirement — at Pleasant Lake. Perry went back to Beloit early. I washed most of the front windows (inside only). Took walk down Lethe Mill Rd — to pump & gun kel. Saw Rose-breasted Grosbeak, Cerulean Blue Warbler, Little Blue Heron, Hummingbird, Mourning Dove, Baltimore Oriole. Wildflowers — Buttercups, yellow & white clone, wild geranium, Hobson's Mayflower, Canada hawkweed, Wood Anemone & others.
Swan in late afternoon.

Last Tuesday (May 26) saw Indigo Bunting at Mary Joerns' in Montana.

Tuesday — Jun 2 – Walked down to 20 –
Worked on breakwater — planted more sedum. Swans in P.M.
Dug worms — tried casting. Saw Big Bass.
Finished "Folie" — I had a dictionary at hand at all times.
Jim & Irene looking at a pontoon boat. It won't work with their new pier as planned with the dbl platform sticking out toward Charles (for landing & take off)

June 1, 1981

First official day of my retirement--at Pleasant Lake.
Took a walk down Liens Mill road to pom-pass grass bed. Saw
Rose-Breasted Grosbeak, Cerulean Blue Warbler, Little Green Heron,
Hummingbird, Mourning Dove, Baltimore Oriole.
Wildflowers--Buttercups, Yellow Sweet Clover, Wild Geranium, Robin's
Ploutain, Canadian Hawkwood, Wood Anenome, and others.

June 2, 1981

Walked down to Highway 20. Worked on breakwater, planted more
Sedum. Swam in afternoon. Dug worms and tried casting. Jim and Irene
looking for a pontoon boat. It won't work with their new pier with the
big L platform sticking out toward Clarks (for landing and takeoff).

July 7, 1981

Took the canvas off the canoe in one piece!! Condition of canoe not too
bad except along the edge--like an egg shell. The inside gunwale is mostly
rotton. Patching weak places along sides--removed some old vanrnish
under gunwales.

Raked weeds from lake bottom and swam.

July 25, 1981

Grandson Geoff was in and out of swimming all day. Made terrific
progress the last day--swam without 'floaties'. Swam underwater, stood
on his hands underwater, etc.

Pruned a lot of bushes on the back hill.

July 16, 1987

Anne (Goodwin) came out today. We had a good swim. Heard about the
honeymoon in Mexico and saw pictures of it and their condo in Atlanta.
She is working on a project here while Matt plays in Florida. She plans to
bring Tom and Todd out on Sunday.

ANNE'S JOURNAL NOTES

I was there for a very intimate
moment in their lives.
Back to the lake now feeling a
little "stopped" by it all. Of
hilltop feels great, beautiful
breeze. Girl scouts are singing to
and echoing each other, Matthew
and here I are off to break fast,
and we are here. For today. And
that's enough.

Pleasant Lake Moment

I am thoroughly enjoying my time spent with Robby and Ben.
They couldn't be more precious and challenging at the same time.
Robby loves the lake and is swimming incessantly at four. Ben would
be content to find every sizable rock in the lake and throw it to see and
hear 'kerplunk'. He's not interested in doing anything else but that.

Evening at Pleasant Lake

The lake seems to offer me the opportunity to write. It's all we have
here...time ticking by, where at home our routines take up all our time.
This morning we packed up the old row boat for a family trip to the
beach across the lake. Ben propelled us over by crying, squirming, and
tantrum revving the entire way there. But I need to back up. Before
we embarked, Matthew invaded a ground wasp's nest and was stung
multiple times. He gallantly fought off his miserableness and after
downing four teaspoons of children's liquid Benadryl, we were off!
To Ben's serenading screams.

Once at the beach, we watched Robby struggle with the concept of sand between his toes (our cottage shoreline is pebbly) and he didn't like it one bit. I watched Matthew become more and more relaxed as the Benadryl kicked in and then...lightning struck. The dark clouds started rolling in and we found ourselves across the lake in a metal row boat with a very iffy oarsman. But, he rallied and started rowing us home. He stopped in the middle of the lake at one point, looking at me in despair and anguish...his bee stings hurt, his carpel tunnel hands were asleep from repetitive rowing and Ben did an unfortunate repeat performance of his boat hysterics. I think we were both ready to help each other jump overboard and abandon both the ship and the boys! A fun day at the beach, thankfully ended.

Solo Visit

I am back, once more, To The Lake. Although this time it is different.... I am alone. It's an amazing thing to have this 24-hour reprieve. I'm hardly sure what to do with myself. For some unexplainable reason, I brought some 'clutter' from home to work through which I've busily set out in circumspect piles—I see myself circling around them nonstop, just as I do at home. Time feels a little awkward. Will it move slowly for a change? This could be a true retreat, perhaps with a couple of canoe paddles for my big social time. Right now I am leaning towards no social time, just me and the cottage. It feels good.

Later—I wish I were brave enough to take myself sailing but it didn't happen. I had a grand time all the same. Actually accomplished a lot yesterday. Wrote in all the journals and laid out an action plan for the Fall as well. I canoed, paddle-boated, swam and enjoyed a fabulous dinner. I'm feeling a little more ready to say goodbye to summer and the cottage... but hard to see a good thing end.

Sketches
On The Lake

Breaking In The Cottage Next Door

It already feels like a warm embrace.
The cool blue of the wicker,
 softened by the orange-oil glow
 of the knotty pine.

Familiar furniture
 that speaks of Kathryn, on her porch,
 where she found lake water solace
 living on the creek, in town.

Fittingly, the set now graces her lake,
 in the cottage of her brother,
 The Cottage Next Door.
Though brother is gone, sister is gone,
 Pleasant Lake traditions
 remain strong.

I am lulled here by the lake.
Always completely charmed and transported.
 Thank you, Kathryn.
 Rest easy about The Cottage Next Door.

My Kayak

My kayak knows the way
As the quiet dusk fills the sky,
we know where life is
             jumping on the lake.

Quickly now to the bay...
        Before the sun drips
            the last drops of light.
    Before the warm call of the cottage
    beckons stronger than
            the chill of the evening breeze.

            It's the magic time.
                    The twinkle time.

    Quickly pass the cottages
            nestled along the shore
                in cottage-row fashion.
    Except for the gaps of missing cottages,
                cottages removed for
            lake houses to come.

            Past the Point, where the water,
        rocks and air skim each other's edge.
            On through the lily pads,
                surrounded by puffs of
                    sunlit sweetened scents
            'come alive' in the evening air.

Look-a turtle, now gone
                    into the deep.
    We know how quickly a
                        turtle moves.

    The cattails wave to greet us,
        The waterlogged limbs
                wait to snag us.
    There's the red-winged black bird
                with one mission-
    to bully the darting brown bird. Day after day,
        is it a game between the two of them?

            Slowly maneuvering through
        the dark, underwater fern,
                I hold my breath.
                    Is he here, is he watching?

Old Blue, the Great heron nonchalantly
                    perched on the white gray limb,
         greets us by not blinking.
Standing with his neck tucked in
                    and his chest puffed out
              he is penguin-like in stature,
                                   full and big.

   We wait. My kayak, me, Old Blue.
         We wait until the
                        other one moves.
                        Who first? He wins.
   Chill sets in, my legs cramp.
         I move and he's off!

In flight, a very thin,
   long-necked, long-footed
         skinny being
beckoning me to the next
              bone naked tree.

      We play this game
                 all around the lake.

      I now know where the big bass
spend their evenings, and how deep a
                     turtle really goes.

      It's been a good night.
              My kayak knows the way home.

Kayak Waltz

A slow sunset dance in
    the middle of the lake.
Our kayaks spin
      as the light changes.

First, a brilliant glow
on the far shore
    illuminating the last row of cottages
edged with dusty blue and deep green reflections.

The sun melts golden
        into the horizon
                as the light shifts to the west
  and transforms into blood red orange.
Highlighted by smoky streaks of gray
                sketched across the sky.

        Billowy puffs turn the lake into
                medallions of magenta
            outlined with pools of shimmering silver.
    Sky meets lake, reflects sky
            and only the kayak edge separates the two.

Night after night, spin after spin
    we do the sunset waltz...
                And remain wonderstruck.

Dragonfly

The dragonfly dance
perpetual motion
    interrupted by a pause
      on a lily pad.

Two face each other
shield-to-shield
    sizing one another up,
      Shall we?

Yes, and they're off
    A burst of flight
dizzyingly performed
    In perfect synchronicity.

A Kayak Pause

Alone, in my
          willow room.
Cool, quiet shade
          enclosed in a canopy
of feathery branches
          delicately brushing
                    the lake...
          As if sipping tea.

A Walk on
Pleasant Lake Road

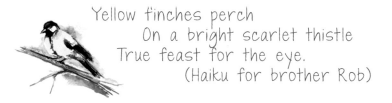

Yellow finches perch
          On a bright scarlet thistle
True feast for the eye.
          (Haiku for brother Rob)

Hello Again

The first night at the lake...
                changes abound.

        There's the large sweeping willow
whose branches we fondly parted
                as we entered the pier,
        now gracefully fallen
                        into the lake.

Someone carved the Secret Passage
                wider than it has ever been.
        But it's still our passage
                        through to the Back Bay
        where life remains the same.

        The bright male red-wing blackbird
chases the nondescript brown female endlessly.

The underground logs
        shifted with the winter chill,
                still quietly beckon.

And then a foreign noise,
            is that a motor coming into the Bay,
                my private chapel?

My kayak moves swiftly
        to greet the boisterous man-boys
                intent on conquering through.

'There is no other side', I tell them,
                'And this is a special spot.
        Engines are not welcome here.'
            I park my kayak
                    facing the sun
    quietly daring them to try and pass.

            They retreat, quieter than they came.
Could it be they hear the birds?

    I remind myself of the
                small darting bird
        chasing the cumbersome crow.

        My beak is sharp and protective.
            As I settle back into the Bay,
    I leave my winter energy behind.
        It is now time to absorb, to listen.
                            To be quiet.

How long will it take me to wean myself
              from the phone?
    Already I've made too many
                  'just checking in' calls.
      It's time to check out.
              To check in with myself.

        I leave the Bay
              and let the wind help carry
          my kayak across the lake.

It feels like deep breathing,
      the awakened rhythm of my stroke
    gliding effortlessly through the
                      rippled water.

To the other *Bay*, Little *Bay*.
              The bay that is slowly becoming
                        a bay no more.
       The new owners of the Point
                   keep clear-cutting.

   Little do they know they
              chop away the home
   of the large snapping turtle,
              and the female Blue heron
   who chooses separate
              living quarters from her mate
                   across the lake.
       She is not around, all due to
              The new view.
       The bare, open view of the lake.

   I turn home, tempted to leave the
              willow draped across our rocky
                   beach and settled into the lake.

              Its repose already feels a part
              of the shoreline.

       Could we build amongst it,
              a natural pier?
       It's good to be back.

Summer Eve

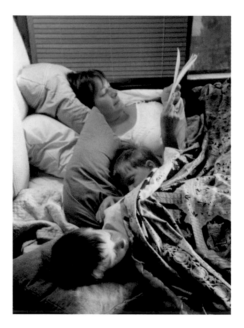

Laughter peals from the Shelter
as the cricket-laden,
scarlet and smoke streaked dusk
drips into night.

Cozy comfort of lake scented boys
entwined like pups
reading on the Big Bed.
Lucky us.

Along The Way in June

Two girls, riding bikes
back and forth
on Pleasant Lake Road.
One stops, puts down her trusty steed
and picks a perfect blade
of long grass.

Pursed lips, she blows hard
and the reed
becomes a siren
answering summer's call.

October In Little Bay

I can't quite grasp my life or
myself back home,
so I've fled to my kayak
and am waiting for
center to come back
as I sit surrounded by
curling lily pads
and raining leaves.

Owl, perched on a limb
        stares down intently at me
looking up at him.
                (Another haiku for Rob)

A Walk on Pleasant Lake Road 2

Wisconsin in late June glory.
Bright blue sky,
white billowy puffs,
blazing afternoon sun,
baked whiffs of pines
buried deep
behind roadside bursts
of soft yellow buttercups
mixed with pale pink
clusters of clover.

Bold scarlet stands of thistle
dot the long summer grasses.
A painted butterfly
holds on tight
as the wind passes through
the bending blades
carrying soft scents of
mid-summer's glory.

Looking Back at August

I have lost the rhythm of the lake.
The restless call of the geese flying
overhead reminds me
            that it isn't June anymore.

August crept in
        with the Back-To-School banners
                blazing and a chill in the air.
    Cottage days are shortening.
            There is a catch in my chest, my breath
getting tighter as I feel summer slipping away.
                Has it been a good one?
    A gift that my children will fondly reopen
            once they are no
                longer confined to 'lake prison'?
                        My one true hope.

Mighty Oaks

One sign of autumn approaching the lake
the acorns dropping all around us.
As they hit the cottage roof,
we feel as if we are in the middle
of a popcorn maker
and cover our heads as we scurry along
with the squirrels busy
collecting their winter bounty.

CRANE TIME

This is the summer of the Sandhill cranes, spotted almost daily on Boy Scout's Point. A pair nested in Little Bay while raising their amber young. I know the Great Blue heron well. The cranes are a surprise. The biggest thrill is watching them come in for a landing. They resemble two lumbering 747s gone awry...lurching, leaning, flapping and at the last moment, touchdown! The surprise comes in watching their ungainly movements a second time and realize they are in perfect synchronicity as they careen through the air.

They allow me to join them. Sitting with my kayak's pointed beak, and the wingspan of my paddle and hat tilted slightly, I try to blend in. Tall and imposing the pair stand side-by-side, as they groom, forage and feed together. Acting singularly until a change occurs. A simple rustle, or quick action brings total unison of movement and long throaty calls. Perfect harmony in motion and voice.

Once assured danger is averted, they go back to tending
themselves. Dusk after dusk, I bask in the familiarity of their
routine and am in awe of their reflective nature. Often as they lean
in towards each other, the silhouette of a large heart appears as
they join heads and gracefully arc their long necks.

The young fledgling is quite a different story. He scolds me endlessly as I enter the bay and he reluctantly takes off into flight. I shake my head, hoping each visit he will stick around just a little longer. And he does. I witnessed one of his first forages into self-feeding. After a patient, watchful shoreline stance, he thrusts his long beak into the tall grass and comes up with a live prize, long-tailed and furry. This unfortunate little guy has now become a practice toy as well as a meal. Again and again, the young crane pokes and stabs his conquest and then dips it into the lake to ease the upcoming long process of swallowing.

When I excitedly returned home to the cottage to share my news of the day with Matthew, he asks with a tinge of disbelief "How long did all this take?" I could not answer.

It is hard to measure Crane time.

THE LOONS

It seems each summer, life on Pleasant Lake offers me an opportunity to make an unusual connection.

One year I hung out with a group of owls canopied in a willow room; we eyed each other almost daily with tilted heads. Another summer, a pair of Sandhill Cranes allowed me into their marshy inner-bog sanctum, a perfect evening cocktail cruise destination in my kayak. Some years, Great Blue Herons play a non-stop game of 'I Am Ahead of You' as they fly from limb to shoreline to limb all around the lake. And if I happen to take the lead....'Squawk, squawk, squawk'.

This year's connection however, is proving to be elusive. Typically
each spring, we are pleased to receive a visiting Loon who pauses
for about a week as he or she heads up to Northern Wisconsin. This
summer, perhaps due to our extreme winter, the Loon chose to stay
on Pleasant Lake. And better yet, somehow found a mate! Loons are
intriguing and not so interested in connecting. They quietly swim
along and the minute I get a tiny bit close, they turn butt-up, dive
deep and swim underwater popping back up clear across the lake.
Their lyrical call is plaintive and yes, just a little bit crazy sounding.
I love the call of the loon. Our pair didn't have much to say on
Pleasant Lake - most likely because they were mated.

I remember a line from a favorite camp song titled, 'The Voyageur',
that talks about 'the call of the lonely Loon'. Although I missed
hearing the calls, I was happy for their contentment. And then
things changed. Now there is only one Loon again swimming alone
at sunset. Nature can be so heartbreaking.

Enter the Girl Scouts. Last night, the girls at Camp
Pottawatomie were having a big time. The lake echoed with the
peals of their laughter, singing and chanting. Girls unabashedly
being girls. As I happily listened to their squeals ringing
from shore to shore, I heard another sound. Our lonely Loon...
trebling along to their joyful noise. Girls then loon. Girls then loon.
Ahh...connection!

Nature did not break any hearts here....She was just being very, very patient and very
busy. We now have baby loons on Pleasant Lake!   In true loon fashion though, they are
not interested in a photo op. (Anne's Journal Entry)

GIRLS NIGHT

"How it feeds my soul to be with such wonderful women."

20+1

Twenty plus one. That's the anniversary marker we celebrated last summer because our brains have become so addled that each and every one of 'us girls' completely missed our twentieth year celebration of gathering at Pleasant Lake. We just let it sail on by. Quietly, maybe even listing a bit, with no reference or beacon of anything extra-ordinary on the horizon.

But not our twenty-first year anniversary. Backing up a bit though....twenty one years ago Matthew's parents generously offered the Shelter for my 36th birthday celebration and the few days surrounding it as well.

That was the birth of Girls Night. At thirty six, with a 4 year old and 1 year old tucked at home, I was positively giddy looking forward to my first child free, friend filled lake escape.

With one of my besties riding shotgun in the first of what became an endless array of minivans (I always said, 'I was a Honda girl in a Mini-Van body' back then), we headed down the highway barely able to contain our whoop whoops! And have felt the same ever since. Although Girls Night guests vary slightly each year, there is a

core group of women who mark their calendars in indelible ink the moment the date is set for the upcoming summer. Jeanne, Lynn, Gail, Dawn, Kathleen, Mary W., Mary S, Lea, Kellie…these are the women who have shared decades of fun together, one night a year on Pleasant Lake. The guest book entries poignantly reveal the passing of time and what twenty-plus years of camaraderie, fun and frolic look like. In our thirties, we outdid ourselves with food preparation, fancy cocktails and thematic decorating. Energy abounded for midnight 'skipper-dippin' and outlandish escapades. We cobbled together flotillas of watercraft (none with motors) to

enjoy endless hours in the middle of the lake with drinks and nibbles floating right along beside us. Swim suits ended up hanging lake down on swim 'noodles' as we shed our inhibitions along with our suits and faced our biggest worry…sinking to the bottom of the lake from laughing too hard. It was exhausting being us. In a very good way.

"Missed naked mid-night noodling,
but our stomachs were fed, souls nurtured
and damn we looked good in our earrings!"

Now most of us are pushing sixty (although Kathleen remains
annoyingly young) and we have mellowed. Gail no longer
transports her entire kitchen to the lake. And we are content with
'ordering out' and 'bringing in' our feasts of choice.

Our motto now is 'less, less, less is more.' We tend to spend more
time on a borrowed pontoon boat (my, we really are grown up!),
puttering around the lake instead of swimming across it.

No more tiki lanterns or transformation of our surroundings,
although we do remember fondly the one year we built an entire
village of hammocks, tents and torches between the lake and
The Shelter just for the sake of extra ambience.

As I prepare for the twenty-second version of Girls' Night it
occurs to me that friendships are a lot like gardens. I consider these
gals my perennial friends. Our roots are deep, drought and flood
resistant, and require minimum care. We have lasted through life's
twists and fates with the typical smatterings of health challenges,
divorces, new marriages, children growing into adults, and parents
growing childlike and still one thing remains the same:

The 'Ahhhs' coming down the hill for that magic moment of
reconnection with each other and with Pleasant Lake.

"All cares and outside world washed
away in the restorative waters of Pleasant Lake"

GIRLS NIGHT GUEST BOOK NOTES

Paging through the years of Girls' Night notations revealed two
major themes---one that the lake is a restorative place and two,
Gail and Lynn forever claim the Shelter corner queen bed known
familiarly as The Big Bed. I must have counted at least forty-seven
times the Big Bed was mentioned. So with that understood, I did
not include those comments in order to have this be a more 'green'
book…less paper. And to give a chance for the lake effect
to shine through.

Friendship at the lake! Joy, laughs, hopes, treats and toasts shared. Skipper dipping to the neon earring dances. Thank you for yet another (4th annual?) girls night out. Soooo pleasant!

5th annual Girls Night. Beautiful flowers, cool lake, feet buffed to perfection (No, Yes, Oh Oh Oh!), great food (what else...) and company. Missed naked mid-night noodling, but our stomachs were fed, souls nurtured and damn we looked good in our earrings! Lovely morning. And the lake was as smooth as glass.

Floral tablecloths, beautiful bouquets from Anne's garden, candles lit all around, wonderful food, all on the most lovely summer evening yet. Did I mention the girls? Some old friends, some new friends—there is something so special about this place that knits it all together. Everybody feels it. Everybody appreciates it. This place puts my world in order. Sunrise service in the bay, a solitary paddle through the mist, a thank you moment to savor. *Lynn is right...life is good.*

A mid-week girls night, the lake is quiet, the girls, of course, are not!! Many laughs, great stories shared (must find Lynn's Scotsman!). The night was cool and stormy which made for a great cottage gathering by the fire and yet another wonderful dinner...what teamwork!

Ah, the Ocean Breeze at Pleasant Lake. What a surprise! The fire was wonderful, such comfort, warmth and some amazing women. *Thanks to all of you!*

Each year a different flavor. Nature adds its own curve this year with constantly 'sustained' wind gusts and white caps on the lake. Lots of outside noise. Inside the fire warmed, the laughs were plentiful, the champagne bottles emptied and the feast memorable. Lots of yawns around 12:30am, and bed was wonderful. Autumn feel at the lake in the middle of July.
Another memory: Kathleen Poked me.

Finally! Back to the lake. Started this Girls Night with Gail's green apple martinis, delicious. Thanks to the vice squad, our sunset cruise was a wealth of laughs and rice, thank goodness. Fire was heavenly, food was bountiful and sleeping weather perfect. Ah...when we're sixty we WILL look back on these years as our prime. Next year we need a cabana boy and let's make it a 3-dayer. A slice of heaven.

So nice to see everybody, toast, catch-up. The lake and sunset were beautiful liquid silver, Sandhill Cranes. So nice to slow down and sun for the day. Thank you! Ahhh...Once I finally got here, instant lake effect. Lovely cocktails, plentiful good food, many laughs. Another fine evening. Gobblin Cobbler, duck duck goose, and perfect water temperature. *Not one ounce of everyday tension left.*

Another fabulous time with great friends, food and song! The rain washed away all of our cares and the champagne made sure of it. Laughter IS always the best medicine. Thank you for the great time. *Another fabulous Girls Night.*

Right now the lake is sparkling, the last to linger. For me the lake and friendship with Anne has been the greatest gift---a healing one...healing the heart in more ways than I can say. Girls Night---well, the laughs as we swam in the middle of the lake---the stories---honestly, these are friends that no time or distance quiets the caring and warmth and rolling laughter. Always good cheer and we know how to DINE. Crab legs, tenderloin, champagne---what could any girl want along with fabulous friends.

Wonderful girls night and day after. Like they said...water was perfect and so refreshing after a hot week. Noodles aplenty and hours of floating and laughing. Love the stormy morning and sunny afternoon. All cares and outside world washed away in the restorative waters of Pleasant Lake.
Ahh yes, thanks Anne for another blissful experience.

Perfect summer day, night, morning. What happens at Pleasant Lake stays at Pleasant Lake. And in our memories. I am bronze. I'm happy and refreshed. I'm grateful for these friends and *21 years of wonderful Girls Night.*

"Back to me!" Kathleen to group

"If that's the best drink

"I don't FEEL it." Mary to Jeanne after sipping on a Mojito

"I'd let you wear it if you had a neck."
Jeanne to Mary regarding topaz necklace

"Things really do change when you turn 40, not necessarily for the better" Jeanne to Gail

"I don't like that."
Gail to Jeanne

"It's getting harder to be us!"
author unknown

"I'm On the Wagon for the next few hours…"
author unknown

"These have to go to the College Next Door." Jeanne delivering drinks

"I'm going to get into the 'nake' …
    It's my signature moon!" *Anne*

it must be mine"
Gail to Jeanne

"Star Lizard Gilly" *Anne referring to Star Gazer Lily?!*

"Twant a cashew?" *Jeanne to Anne*

I'm getting ready for the accident. *upon docking the pontoon*

Mind the gap!
upon entering the pontoon

"What am I doing?" *Jeanne asks wandering past*

"We were drinking", *Anne's swift response*

Where's you trombone NOW?

I don't need any more opportunities
to practice tolerance, Thank You.
Lynn, celebrating 50 to group:

"Read my Tiara!"

*Do we have an open
bottle of champagne?"
"Oldest question ever*

*You shouldn't squish
up your face like
that so early in the
morning.*

DAY IS DONE

TAPS ON THE LAKE

Did I mention sound travels on the lake? Sitting on the shore, pier or even our deck, I am privy to conversations floating by on a daily basis. Here is what didn't register one summer. The lake carries sound away from our cottages as well.

Enter eleven year-old Rob Goodwin at the end of the school year in possession of a new challenge for the summer...learning to play the trumpet. We all suffered through that summer of sour notes in small quarters gritting our teeth. One evening, I escaped to my kayak before he started to dutifully practice.

Beautifully situated in Little Bay, I was just beginning to exhale when I heard, as if through a mega-phone, the beginning 'off' notes enthusiastically trying to be a scale. I made a wake all the way home. I was mortified that we had been such inconsiderate lake neighbors.

Rob made up for it. Ever since his first foray to overnight camp, where he was tapped to play Taps for evening song, Rob has graced the lake with a Taps serenade at the end of the pier at the end of each day. The first years we held our collective breath for each note to ring true. Over the years Rob has evolved into a serious jazz trumpeter and soloist. As his prowess on the trumpet grew, his Taps transformed into a haunting soliloquy. We are probably the only lake in Wisconsin where the shoreline erupts in applause in celebration of day being done. Always a proud and poignant moment of gratitude.

Path to the Shelter from the Cottage Next Door.

Path to the Cottage Next Door

Our Beacon.

The Big Bed at the Shelter.

'Lake Ready' at the Cottage Next Door.

The Magic Time.

→

 1. Camp Juniper Knoll

 2. Submerged 'Box With Rocks'

 3. Secret Passage

 4. Corn Dog Island

 5. Back Bay

 6. Cranes Nesting

 7. Beaver Lodge

 8. Turtle Bay

 9. Arrowhead Point

 10. Cottages

 11. Sandy Beach

 12. Camp Pottawatomie Hills

 13. Little Bay

14. Boy Scout Point

15. LaGrange Public Beach

1.

15.

14.

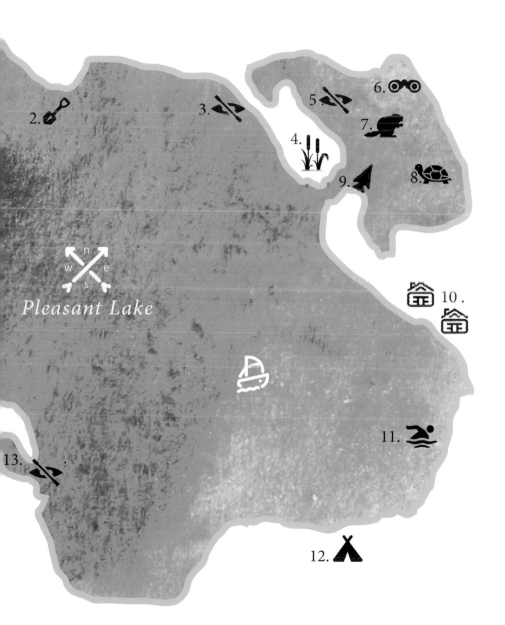

Pleasant Lake

BE THE PAUSE

The Shelter, The Cottage Next Door and Hilltop are some of the last standing original cottages remaining on the lake. People actually comment on boats going by ... "look there's a shack!"…or "look little houses too!" (not realizing sound carries very well over water). The actual word 'cottage' has become obsolete in our vocabulary. During my first Pleasant Lake visits I travelled a mile to place phone calls standing outside on the edge of a highway. And of course, since then, technology has crept its way onto the shores of Pleasant Lake. Cell phones, hot spots, laptops now accompany us but do not hold center court. We still relish our routines and time spent connecting. This little book will help remind us of our ideal cottage life. And hopefully will inspire visits on these pages often. Please come back to the lake, anytime.

←⟨⟨⟨

The Shelter Check Out List

Please –

☐ Wipe down all surfaces including bathroom

☐ Sweep Floor throughout cottage

☐ Organize refrigerator, wipe down remove perishables

☐ Set out Fresh towels, remove old ones

☐ Make Big Bed taut (rumpled doesn't work!)

☐ Empty Trash Containers. Take trash to Hill

☐ Close all windows, except back bedrooms

☐ Tidy up Waterfront – boats, life jackets, paddles, noodles secure

☐ Check all candles, Fires, Oven are OFF

☐ close and lock Doors

☒ come Back Soon

Please leave cottage better than you found it and check-in ready for next guests.
Thank You!

Tiny Kitchen Cooking

BOYVILLE RECIPES

Tiny kitchen staples...these few spices work their magic together in most of the following recipes. Big flavors for small spaces.

Boyville Breakfast

Fryin' Bacon

@ One simple ingredient makes our bacon sing at Pleasant Lake:
a well-seasoned, cast iron skillet. A must have.

@ I like to cut my bacon in half and fry it. I find it goes farther and is easier
to manage. I tend to use half the package at a time, depending on number of
hungry boys.

Cast Iron Skillet / 3 lb.package Thick Slab Bacon.

Fry bacon over medium/medium high heat turning often until
maple-colored crisp with a chew left in it. Important not to overcook,
especially when it is warming while people are still sleeping.
Line a jelly roll pan with paper towels, and place fried bacon in warm
(200 deg.) oven making sure paper towel and bacon pieces are not
anywhere near heat source. Reserve a couple of tablespoons of bacon
grease for scrambled eggs.

"The Bomb" French Toast

@ We recycle a lot at Pleasant Lake. Use every last bit of everything to
avoid having to leave the lake to drive to the store. One morning, I decided
to put my skillet full of bacon grease to good use.

Cut thick slabs of left-over **French or Italian bread.** Let dry on counter
if 'too fresh'. Nine or so pieces. Crack three **eggs** into a shallow baking or
pie pan. Loosely beat, add a combined cup of **Half and Half** and
One Percent Milk (both are always in our refrigerator, any milk will do).
Sprinkle generous amounts of **cinnamon powder,** tablespoon of **white
sugar,** and a sprinkle of **sea salt.** Loosely whisk together, until combined.
Heat bacon grease in cast iron skillet. While heating fat, start dipping
and soaking first batch of bread slices. When well soaked, hold piece
above pan to drop excess egg mixture, then place in heated grease in
skillet. Brown both sides until toasty brown, this can require more than
one turn and then place single-layered on jelly roll pan lined with paper
towel. Continue cooking all pieces. When pan is full, sprinkle with
raw sugar granules on top and place in warm oven and let caramelize.
Serve with heated real **maple syrup.**

Grandma Anne's Scrambled Eggs

@ Conejitos is our go to restaurant in Milwaukee, and their green salsa is a kitchen staple. Great heat, great fresh flavor. Maybe they will ship?

In another cast iron skillet, generously greased with reserved bacon grease, crack eight to twelve **eggs** and stir by scraping the bottom (kind of shoveling eggs towards the sides really) of pan as eggs begin to cook. When mostly cooked, add two generous tablespoons of **Conejitos Fresh Salsa Verde,** two handfuls or so of shredded cheese-- **four cheese Mexican.** (note-Not the Mexican Taco Seasoned shredded cheese). Stir until all is melted and soft scrambled. Sprinkle generously with **fresh ground pepper.** No salt needed with zesty green salsa.

Breakfast Burritos

@ I am never one to wait around for sleepyheads to awake at the lake. Too much is happening out there and I want to be smack in the middle of morning's glory. So, leaving a tray of breakfast burritos warming in the oven works for me. And the guys.

@ The secret to any great soft flour taco, quesadilla, or burrito: Flaming your tortilla directly on the gas burner or grill prior to anything else. The high heat and little char releases flavor and gives a little more texture to the tortilla as well.

Breakfast burritos usually consist of **ham, Mexican shredded cheese, egg** and again, **fresh green salsa, red salsa,** and flamed **large tortillas.** But, if no ham, then any left-over meat on hand. Steak, pork, chicken…I've even thrown in hard salami when it was my only option. **Sour Cream** and **fresh cilantro** options finish the mix.

Start with flaming both sides of the tortillas. When air pockets puff up its time to flip. I prefer a toasty brown, with a little black around some edges on one side, softly warmed on other side. Set aside stacked soft-side up on jelly roll pan. Cover loosely with foil. Next saute meat until warm Set aside.

Heat bacon grease or butter in large skillet, crack eggs directly into heated fat and scrape pan bottom as eggs cook. When eggs are softly scrambled, add green salsa and a couple of handfuls of Mexican shredded cheese. Add pepper. Add sautéed meat and cook until cheese is melted. Spread individual tortilla with green salsa, red salsa, sour cream (if desired), and add egg mixture to one side, fold up bottom, roll to close, and carefully set on jelly roll pan. After burritos are prepared, put in warm (200) oven. Serve with sides of salsas, sour cream, and cilantro for fresh toppings. Loosely tent with foil while keeping warm.

If non-meat is desired, I often add a leftover cooked medley of potatoes, corn and onions. If non-egg is desired, I will do ham and cheese, or a strange but tasty combo of sautéed ham and wild **grape jelly.** But always, first, on a flamed tortilla.

Make Your Own Meal

@ *There is something fun about being in charge of your own food experience. We do a lot of 'make your own meals' at Pleasant Lake: Build Your Own Sandwich platters, Taco Bar, and Steak-on-A-Stick are perennial Boyville favorites.*

Build Your Own Sandwich Platter

It's all about providing lots of options for building tasty sandwiches from a platter. It starts with an enthusiastic visit to the local deli department, and purchasing sliced ham, roast beef, turkey or chicken, hard salami, lacy Swiss, Colby, Jalapeño and Cheddar cheese. From the fresh produce section romaine lettuce, ripe tomatoes, sweet onion, fresh basil and tricolor peppers. Condiments include mayo, sweet/sassy mustard, olive oil, balsamic vinegar, zesty Bread and Butter pickle chips. Bread options—an array of sliced Italian, Kaiser Buns, and French Baguette. All presented on large platters for people to create their own personal sandwich masterpiece.

Taco Bar

@ *The foundation of a fabulous taco bar includes well-seasoned meat and a large spread of fresh ingredients to build an endless variety of tacos. And then of course, the pre-flamed tortillas. Our lake taco bars consist of using two meat bases:* **ground turkey** *and* **roasted chicken.**

" My dearest Anne fed the troops over, and over, and over with love and tacos."

The Meat

....

@ *I'll never forget, on a first sleepover, an enthusiastic Cody walking into the kitchen and going all crest-fallen when he saw the onion cooking. "My mom doesn't put onions in our taco meat," he told me thoroughly concerned. "This is how we do it at Pleasant Lake", was my pat answer for all queries, which worked magic!*

In cast-iron skillet brown chopped garlic and diced large **sweet onion** in a couple of tablespoons of **butter** and **olive oil** each. Once the onions are nicely browned, add two to three lbs. of regular ground turkey (85/15 percent fat ratio, fat adds good stuff!) and brown. Remove liquid and discard. Add two to three packets of **El Paso regular taco seasoning,** (I usually use one hot version). Add water as directed. Stir. Add half-bottle of **La Victoria Green Taco Sauce** and simmer low on top of stove for at least an hour, stirring often. When thickened, place in casserole with lid and keep warm in oven. Next, debone into bite size pieces one or two **whole roasted chickens** (purchased roasted from deli) and place in casserole with a lid. Sprinkle with **fresh lime juice** (one lime), a couple handfuls of **fresh cilantro,** McCormick Hot Shot pepper mix, two cans of **diced green chilies,** two cans of **green Enchilada Sauce or Salsa Verde sauce,** and some **Conejito's green salsa** (that again!) and mix well. Bake covered at 300 until chicken is 'stewy' and most of the liquid has baked into the chicken. Keep warm in oven along with ground turkey meat.

133

The Rest Of The Stuff

Skillet Corn: Use **left-over corn** from the cob or a large bag of **frozen corn.** Start with ½ a cup of water, couple of generous tablespoons **raw sugar** and **butter** each, and generous teaspoon of **salt** to a sauce pan and bring to a boil. Add the corn, cover until a furious boil, uncover, and continue the medium hard boil until all liquid is reduced. Sprinkle madly with **cracked pepper** throughout the reduction. Add more salt if needed. Let stay warming on the stove top, scraping pan bottom occasionally. No cover, unless tilted for steam to escape.

Fresh Guacamole

Scoop three to four well-ripened **avocados** into a mixing bowl. Add juice from half **lime.** Sprinkle with Hot Shot and Garlic Pepper. Add heaping spoonful each of Conejito's **green salsa** and Pace Chunky Medium **red salsa.** (Of course, any red and green salsa will do, I am just sticking to the Pleasant Lake version). Mix all, coarsely cutting through with knife and back of spoon until smooth and a little chunky. Smush clear wrap directly on guacamole in bowl, to remove all air pockets, then clear wrap bowl tight, place in fridge.

Chop fine and place in small bowls:

Sweet Onion, Tomatoes, and **Cilantro**

Shredded lettuce and shredded **four-Mexican cheese** (large bowls)

Sour Cream, red salsa, and **green salsa** (small bowls)

'On 'The Border' **Tortilla Chips** (large bowl)

Flame **taco-size flour tortillas** (family pack of 20 to start) on burner and keep wrapped in foil. (I collect old fashion bun warmers and keep foil packet heated while adding flamed tortillas) Set all ingredients on table with tortillas and meats nearest the plates. Then corn, then cold ingredients. Add a tray of sliced **watermelon** at end.

Steak-On-A-Stick-Dinner

@ The first ingredient might be hard to come by. I happened upon a used Chinese appetizer table grill at a yard sale and picked it up for a dollar. The return investment of that dollar in pure dining joy is immeasurable. Hands-down favorite go-to lake dinner for kids ranging from ages 2 to 62. If no 'bobo platter' table grill, any table hibachi will do.

Start with large packet of thinly sliced **sirloin steak** (3 lbs.). Marinate in following ingredients (or bottled Sesame/Ginger sauce if easier): Pour into a large zip-lock bag: a quarter-inch of **soy sauce,** eighth-inch **sesame oil,** generous dashes of **red or sherry vinegar,** dashes of **ginger powder,** Hot Shot pepper mix, garlic pepper, a couple of tablespoons **raw sugar** or **honey** and place meat in one or two bags of marinade and let sit for at least a couple of hours. Sear meat on grill both sides and remove. Should be seared outside, pink inside. (3-4 mins. max) Let cool on platter. Tear pieces of steak into bite-size pieces and place two or three each on wooden skewer. Set platter of skewed meat aside.

Roasted Corn

*@ I always try to keep a large bag of **frozen corn** on hand, **or** of course love using **left-over corn** from the cob which I often freeze as well. Who knew you could roast frozen corn?*

Preheat oven to 425. Rinse corn under water until loose and drain well. Place in bowl with tablespoon-plus of **olive oil** (light, for roasting), two tablespoons **raw sugar,** generous **salt** and **pepper.** Mix well. Place single layer in jelly roll pan and roast about 5-7 minutes, stirring once or twice. Some kernels will be brown, others lightly caramelized, others just cooked through. Place in casserole serving dish and keep warm in oven, loosely covered to let steam escape.

Bow Tie Pasta

@ *Simple, simple, simple. But kids love it. Big kids too.*

@ *Now that I am thinking about this, perhaps next time I'll offer fresh basil as a side. Basically, build your own pasta in your bowl.*

Cook one package **Farfalle** as directed for 'al dente'. Drain, put generous hunk of **butter** /tablespoon-plus extra-virgin **olive oil** in hot pasta pot. Put pasta back in pot stirring through melted butter/ oil mixture. Sprinkle generously with Morton's Nature Seasoning Salt and McCormick Garlic Pepper. Hot Shot sprinkle to taste. Place in serving bowl, with accompanying small bowls of shredded **parmesan** and **olive/sun-dried tomato tapenade**.

Nanny's Cucumber Salad

@ *My grandmother's "Edith Barber Cookbook" from the 1940's has been a family bible. Nanny enjoyed a fresh cucumber salad. Again simple yet so tasty. And speaks 'summer' right out loud.*

Peel and thinly slice two to three med/large **cucumbers**. Place bottom layer of cucumber in wide bowl, sprinkle with **apple-cider vinegar, raw sugar, salt** and **pepper** and repeat with next cucumber layer. Again and again. After last layer, wrap and chill in refrigerator.

Ice Cream Sundae Bar

This barely needs explaining. Gather all and every component you can think of to make an ice cream bar tasty and fun. Start with offering cone or dish option, several ice cream flavors, chocolate/ caramel/strawberry sauces, fresh assorted berries, bananas, cherries, nuts, Redi-Whip (fun in a can) and let 'er rip.

FAMILY LAKE RECIPES

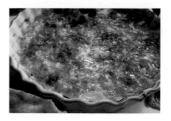

Ruth French's Vidalia Onion Dip

@ *Ruth was a bestie of my mother's and family best friend. She was the quintessential 'gathering hostess'...fed a crowd outrageously good food, with grace and ease.*

Oh my, with this dish, people request an IV drip. And so simple!! One very large (or two small) **Vidalia Onion(s)** coarsely chopped, one cup **Baby Swiss** shredded, One cup **Hellman's Real Mayonnaise** ....mix all together. Mixture should be thick onion/cheesy. Season with bits of Natures Seasoning, Garlic Pepper, Hot Shot. Spread in lightly buttered pie dish, or quiche dish, (shallow baking pan) sprinkle with shredded **Parmesan** and **paprika**. Bake at 350 until golden brown and bubbly on top...about 30 minutes. Let set a bit, very hot when out of the oven. Serve with **assorted crackers**.

Sloppy Joe's

@ *One of our sons' favorites...so much so, when Ben graduated from high school he made a Facebook invite to his graduation party promoting his Mom's homemade BBQ...to all 200 plus of his nearest and dearest. It took me years to feel like making it again after May 2012.*

First, the ingredients: Purchase 3lbs **ground turkey** (85/15 fat ratio). Large **green pepper,** fresh **garlic** cloves, large **Vidalia onion,** six **celery** stalks, **tomato paste** (2 small cans), Nature Seasoning Salt, McCormick Garlic Pepper, McCormick Hot Shot (or tobacco sauce), large bottle Hunts **Ketchup,** Sweet and Sassy **Mustard,** Red Wine **Vinegar, Worchester Sauce, Brown Sugar,** Real **Maple Syrup.**   ⟫⟫⟶

Lightly sauté finely chopped garlic cloves (3) in olive oil and butter melted in cast iron skillet, add chopped onion and sauté until slightly caramelized, add chopped green pepper and chopped celery, sauté all vegetables until well browned and soft. Add more butter or oil if needed. Add turkey and brown well. Remove liquid in skillet. Sprinkle generous tablespoons of seasoning salt and garlic pepper, plus generous teaspoon plus of Hot Shot. Add tomato paste, stir throughout meat until well coated with paste and spices.

Add almost half of bottle of ketchup, half of small bottle of mustard, a couple of sprinkles of vinegar, tablespoon or two of Worchester, couple tablespoons of brown sugar, tablespoon of maple syrup. Mix well. Add a little (½ cup) water to start the simmering process. Simmer slowly on stove top for a couple of hours, adding water as needed to keep from burning or becoming too thick too soon. Water will cook away. Serve on toasted slider buns or sweet Hawaiian rolls.

Purple Cabbage Slaw with Granny Smith Apple

@ *This slaw is fun....beautiful and appeals to all age groups with the added sweet tartness of the Granny Smith.*

Coarsely chop **purple cabbage,** grate peeled **apple** (ratio one small head cabbage, one large apple) and mix quickly in the bowl so the apple stays bright. Sprinkle generously with McCormick Garlic Pepper.

Mix premade slaw dressing with a large spoonful of **mayo,** a shot of **honey** and coat lightly. Serve with side bowl of crumbled **Blue Cheese** for individual preference. If no slaw dressing, combine half-a-cuppish **Hellman's Real Mayonnaise,** tablespoon **honey** and strong dashes of **apple cider vinegar,** stir together, taste should be tangy with a touch of sweet, (seasoning will come from the peppered slaw), and add to bowl.

@ Labor Day has always been a great blend of family and friends gathering to toast summer good bye. We pile on to Cousin Lee's pontoon, tootle around with snacks and tasty concoctions and then after sunset has made its splash, enjoy what I call 'platter dinners' at The Shelter. Typically with a fire blazing, since sometimes the chill has already set in a bit. And it's always good to glow.

Roasted Lemon Chicken with Orzo

@ Another favorite kitchen treasure...large clay/enamel-coated roaster with lid. (Brand name Romertopf) I found mine with a perfect patina and do not have to soak it before roasting. However that is the suggested method, so if new, soak roaster first in water.

Roasted Chicken:

Preheat Oven to 425. I either roast one large (5lbs-plus) **organic chicken** or 2 small ones (4lbs-minus, turned sideways in pot). Squeeze three **lemons,** marinate breast side down in lemon juice in roasting pot, turning occasionally for at least 30 minutes. Save lemon halves. Coat chicken with **Olive Oil** (light, for roasting), then rub entire bird with **kosher salt,** and McCormick **garlic pepper.** Insert lemon halves in chicken cavity. Finish chicken breast-side down (key to moist chicken) in lemon juice, place in oven uncovered. Roast for 50-60 minutes (depending on browning and chicken size) then add cover and continue for 30-40 minutes until chicken is done. Remove from oven, and let sit in juice covered on counter. ⟫⟶

Orzo with Roasted Tri-Colored Peppers and Onions:

@ *Love, love, love the satisfying texture and flavor of this concoction.*
I prefer big, hearty orzo (which sounds like an oxymoron since Orzo is a tiny
rice-like pasta). RiceSelect brand in large plastic jar is my favorite.

Vegetables (may do ahead):

Pre-heat oven to 425. Mince 3 large cloves of **garlic** and set in large mixing
bowl soaking in **Olive Oil** with generous **Garlic Pepper** sprinkles.

Dice in small pieces **one each-yellow, red and orange pepper** and one large
Vidalia onion. Place all vegetables in bowl and toss with garlic/oil mixture
until lightly coated. Spread mixture on jelly roll pan and roast until well
browned and soft, occasionally scraping and re-spreading. I roast until
some pieces have a nice charred finish.

Set aside mixture in bowl with all the pan oils and scrapings and cover.

Orzo:

Cook half of one of those jars, or a full box/bag of regular orzo,
per 'al dente' instruction. (Simmer 9 minutes at most.)
Drain orzo quickly in the sink.

Put roasted vegetable mixture into the warm pasta pot coating the pan
bottom and re-add orzo to pot. Mix thoroughly lightly lifting and
stirring. Add one package of **fresh mozzarella 'pearls'** or cut up chunks,
plus at least half a container of **shredded parmesan** and lift and stir
gently. Cheese will begin to melt. Add a touch of salt and Hot Shot. Place
paper towel over pot, put lid on top of paper towel and let rest on stove.
After chicken has composed in the pot, grab a large platter and carve
chicken and place pieces on platter. Take warm lemon au jus (or heat up
au jus on stove top in small saucepan) and spoon generously onto the
orzo mixture.

Add chopped fresh basil to orzo. Place Orzo mixture next to chicken on
platter. Sprinkle Orzo with fresh shredded Parmesan. Add cooked fresh
organic **spinach** next to orzo. Make sure it is just past wilted, still bright
green, cook in shallow water, lifting occasionally to turn, and keep in
strainer over pot until it is dry, season as desired. Spoon remaining au jus
over the entire platter…chicken, orzo and spinach. Beautiful!

Nancy's Party Steak Platter

@ *This 1960's recipe goes against all good food sense....who would put ketchup and a fine sirloin steak in the same recipe, or even the same sentence? It's happening here and trust me, it is crazy good.*

Ask your butcher for a four to five inch **Sirloin steak** (about 4lbs), special cut, hopefully Prime meat or Choice, highest grade piece of meat available. To clarify, this is not a roast but a steak and you want it that thick. Bring to room temperature before roasting.

Pre-heat oven to 425. Preheat grill to high also. Rub one side of steak with **olive oil.** Mix together heaping teaspoons of **garlic pepper, paprika** and **raw sugar** and rub on oiled side. When grill is 'sear' ready place naked side down for two minutes, and then flip, add oil and spices to seared side. Sear another two minutes. Flip once more for quick finish and remove.

In a bowl, mix one cup **ketchup,** three teaspoons **lemon juice,** tablespoon **Worchester,** one large **Vidalia onion** grated, and one **green pepper** grated. Spread mixture on top of steak. Place in shallow roasting pan. Roast uncovered for 45 minutes for medium rare (about 15 minutes per pound). Let sit tented with foil.

Steak Picante Sauce:

In small saucepan, melt 3 tblsp. **butter,** combine ½ cup Sweet and Spicy **barbeque sauce,** ¼ cup Sassy Sweet **mustard,** 2 tblsp. **Worchester** sauce, sprinkle Hot Shot and heat well. Before serving, warm sauce, and stir in ½ a cup or so of **half and half, or heavy whipping cream,** heat just before simmer.

Slice steak thin, straight cut, arrange on platter. Drizzle warm sauce over steak, sprinkle generously with **fresh parsley.**

Fresh Asparagus

@ *Luckily, we have an Asparagus Stand on Pleasant Lake Road. Actually it's a cooler on the side of the road with an 'honor system' jar. We contribute to that jar often.*

Start by snapping the ends off the **asparagus.** (One bunch).

Place asparagus in skillet on stove and cover with cold water.

Add some **salt** and **sugar** to the water. Bring to a boil uncovered, let simmer 4-8 minutes dependent on width of stalk, remove and drain, asparagus should be bright green and a little bendy. Place back in warm pan, season lightly with Salt and Pepper, or Nature's Seasoning, tent lightly. Place on platter next to roasted vegetables.

Roasted Corn, Butternut Squash, Onion Medley

There is something about this trio roasted that just works.
Pre-make this and reheat to add to platter. Preheat oven to 425.
Sometimes I add a small clove of **garlic** chopped, sometimes not. If so,
place garlic in bottom of mixing bowl drenched in **olive oil,** add Garlic
Pepper, let stand. **Dice Vidalia or Sweet Onion** into medium bite-size
chunks, peel and cube raw **butternut squash,** (or much better, purchase
prepared cubes oven ready) and add both to bowl. Lightly coat. Place in
Jelly Roll pan. Roast until caramelized…browned and cooked through.
About 30 minutes. Scrape, turn and separate half way through and once
again before removing from oven. Ten minutes before done, use a
package of **frozen corn or** left-over fresh **off the cob,** coat with **olive
oil** and tablespoon **raw sugar, salt and pepper** in bowl. Spread out on
separate jelly pan and place in the oven. Caramelize slightly, about 5-7
minutes total). Add corn to the squash/onion and place medley in
casserole, reheat in warm oven uncovered while steak is composing.
Mix in chopped fresh **basil or cilantro** before placing on platter.

Favorite Breakfasts

Egg on Toast

ⓐ *It's all about the toast. And then there's the special best-ever Wisconsin cheese melted on a fried-to-order egg, and finally an organic egg. That, plus toast with butter, wild grape jelly or buckwheat honey and a little fresh fruit garnish and voila!...a perfect lake breakfast. Well, perfectly perfect would have some fresh corn-dusted, pan fried 'pan' fish on the side.*

ⓐ *Pleasant Lake toast is Pepperidge Farm Very Thin White Bread. Please buy a loaf every time you see one just to keep the product coming. I don't think it's very politically correct these days...like Jiffy Peanut Butter (my choice) and I'm afraid Pepperidge Farm will ruin everything and add whole grain. This was my grandmother's bread of choice for toast and tea sandwiches. Not to be messed with.*

Fry **eggs** softly in butter in cast iron skillet. Turn and grate generous amount of Wisconsin's special **Bellavitano Santori Merlot Cheese** over eggs. Turn off heat and cover, let sit while toasting bread. Cheese will melt fully, eggs will be over-easy. Place on buttered piece of toast.

Serve additional toast with Grandma Kayo's turned into Grandma Anne's homemade **wild grape jelly** or **local buckwheat honey.** Add fresh peach slice, orange slice or berry medley on the side.

Fresh Lake Pan Fish, Corn-dusted and Pan-Fried

ⓐ *When the Blue Gills (or other pan fish) show up for breakfast, it is a special treat. A person who fishes, and knows how to clean and filet a fish properly must show up first.*

In a small Ziploc bag, combine equal heaping spoonfuls of **flour** and **yellow cornmeal,** generous dashes of Natures Seasoning and Hot Shot sprinkles.In a shallow dish, soak fish filet in **half and half or milk** with tablespoon fresh **lemon juice.** ⟫⟶

Heat a mixture of **butter** and **olive oil** in cast iron. Shake extra liquid off fish, place in bag and coat well. Sautee until golden brown and flip…altogether the fish should cook five minutes max…they cook very quickly.

Remove from skillet, place on jelly roll pan or cookie sheet lined with paper towel, squeeze fresh lemon over filets, add salt and pepper to taste, keep warming in oven until breakfast is served.

Nancy's Southern Pancakes

@ *I like to cook, but am not much of a baker. Which is why you do not see exact amounts in my cooking instructions. I don't use them. However, in this instance I do. This was a favorite pancake of ours growing up. And has become the pancake of choice at the Lake as well. I love the flavor of the corn drenched in pure maple syrup. I think these would be considered lighter in gluten but personally am not interested. I have cocktail napkins that state …"For God's sake, let's eat some gluten!" So if you're one who enjoys a little carb now and then, give these a try.*

Sift ½ cup **flour,** 3 teaspoons **baking powder** and 1 teaspoon of **salt.** Set aside. Add ½ cup of boiling water to ½ cup of **yellow corn meal,** plus 1 tablespoon of **sugar** in mixing bowl and beat well. Add flour to cornmeal mixture, plus ¼ cup of milk slowly, beat well by hand. Slowly pour in ¼ cup of heated **butter.**

Fold in 2 **eggs,** well beaten. Heat lightly oiled skillet to water-drop sizzle. Drop by spoonful and cook to bubbly, dry-edged and flip.

Heat 100% **Pure Mable Syrup** in saucepan, butter optional. (but not for my husband, it's in his 'need' category…my mom used to melt a chunk of butter in the syrup, tasty!)

Tasty Concoctions

Summer Bar Larder

@ *Mixology is another crayon box altogether. And I love playing with it, especially with the fresh colors and tastes of summer. This is what I like to keep on hand at all times-*

Fresh lemon, lime, orange, blueberries, basil, cucumber and mint.

Vodka, Gin, Rum, Tequila and Bourbon

Chandon Ginger Liquor, St. Germaine, Aperol, Bitters. Ameretto, Kahlua, Club Soda, Bitter Lemon (old mixer, very hard to find, try Polar brand), Tonic, Ginger Beer, Cranberry Juice, Grapefruit Juice, Simply Lemonade, Simply Limeade, Cristalino Brut Cava, (by the case, it is my house wine), a nice crisp White and a pleasing Red.

Sparklings

Champagne cocktails are signature at Pleasant Lake.

We like to make them refreshing in large red wine glasses with ice.

To the champagne base we add:

    Aperol with large orange slice

    Chandon Ginger with lemon slice

    St. Germaine with lemon twist and dash of club soda (or not)

    Dash of Bitters with twist of choice

Special Requests

Summer On The Pier

Vodka or Gin, fresh lime juice, Chandon Ginger, Bitter Lemon
(or equal parts lemonade and tonic), dash of club soda on top.
Garnish with Lime, Mint and Blue Berries. Deliver to pier.

Fresh Margarita

Good to make a pitcher full.   Start with juicing six limes, add
15 second-count pour of Tequila.   Add 3 capfuls of Amaretto
(or Cointreau), fill mixture and pitcher with ice, and pour over fresh
limeade.   Serve with fresh lime. (Infuse tequila with fresh whole
jalapeños to make snappy Margie, muddle fresh basil for garnish on
this version).

GIRLS NIGHT SAMPLE MENU

"Always good cheer and we know how to dine!
Crab legs, tenderloin, champagne."

Gail's Crab Dip

1 8oz Philadelphia Cream Cheese softened
1 Tbsp. prepared horseradish
Hellman's Mayo
1 can crab meat
1 package small shrimp
Cavendars Greek Seasoning

Mix mayo with the cream cheese to a paste consistency. Add drained crab and a little more mayo. Add horseradish and shrimp and mayo until mixture is smooth. Season to taste with Cavendars and more horseradish as desired. Cover and chill in refrigerator, may be made a day ahead. Serve with assorted crackers. Good to double recipe. Or just make a vat of it.

Lea's Grilled Bacon-Wrapped, Bourbon-Glazed Shrimp

16 pieces of bacon
16 uncooked large shrimp, peeled and deveined
8 bamboo skewers
⅓ cup of Dijon mustard
5 tablespoons bourbon
Vegetable oil
2 tablespoons dark brown sugar

Wrap bacon around shrimp. Thread two shrimp per skewer.
Mix mustard and bourbon in small bowl. Brush on shrimp, let chill for a while in baking dish.
Prepare grill at medium high heat brushed with oil. Press 1 Tbsp. sugar through sieve over shrimp, turn and repeat. Let stand 15 minutes. Grill shrimp cooked through about 3 minutes.
(This is a low country recipe that Lea switched bacon for the suggested thin prosciutto. Really delicious substitute although she warns of an 'interesting grilling experience!" Beware!)

Lynn's Fresh Corn Salad

@ *This recipe is perfect for what to do with left over ears of corn in the pot.*
Refrigerate and the next day remove corn from cob.

3 or more ears cooked corn, removed from cob

Diced ripe tomatoes, seeded (grape, cherry, Roma,) ⅓ ratio to corn

Diced sweet onion (equal amount to tomato)

2 tablespoons White Balsamic Vinegar

Raw Sugar

Fresh Basil (torn)

Salt and Pepper to taste

Mix sugar and vinegar in mixing bowl, add corn, onion and tomato.
Toss and chill. Add basil right before serving and add
salt and pepper as desired.

Mary's Melon Prosciutto Mozzarella Basil Skewers

½ cup of olive oil

⅓ cup fresh basil leaves

1 shallot loosely cut up

1 cantaloupe, seeded and scooped into melon balls or cut in small wedges

Small mozzarella balls (one package)

6 thin slices prosciutto, cut in half lengthwise

8 bamboo skewers

Prepare cantaloupe. Alternate one melon, prosciutto, moz ball,
prosciutto again, melon again on skewer. Puree together shallot and
olive oil and basil until shallot is finely chopped. Drizzle on top of
plattered skewers and add cracked pepper. So fresh and delish.

Dawn's Heirloom Tomato Lettuce Wraps

@ *A Caprese salad in your hand! Take* **romaine lettuce leaves,** *fill
individually with heirloom* **tomato** *slices, fresh mozzarella chunk,* **basil**
leaves and drizzle with **Balsamic vinegar.** *Dawn likes to spread some of
Trader Joe's cilantro salad dressing on the lettuce as well and often adds*
bacon *strips for more 'oomph'.*

Anne's Grilled Tenderloin with Béarnaise Sauce

@ At home, I follow Ina Garten's roasted tenderloin recipe. Basically you smear the loin with butter and roast it at extremely high heat. At the lake, keeping the teeny tiny kitchen cool is preferable so we jack up the grill for tenderloin and forego the butter!

1 Beef Tenderloin (4 lbs.)

Extra Virgin Olive Oil

Coarse salt and fresh ground pepper

It is best to use direct (hot) and indirect heat on the grill whether you have gas or charcoal. Rub tenderloin with oil and salt and pepper. Sear over hot grill each side until caramelized (about 3 minutes a side), and then grill covered over indirect heat for approximately 25 minutes for medium rare. Let stand on platter, tented for at least 10 minutes.

Béarnaise Sauce:

3 Tbsp. tarragon vinegar   ½ tsp salt

3 Tbsp. water   Dash paprika

3 onion slices   4 Tbsp. butter   4 egg yolks, slightly beaten

In small sauce pan bring water, vinegar, onion slices to boiling. Discard onion. Into egg yolks in top of double boiler, gradually stir vinegar mixture. Add salt, paprika. Cook over hot water stirring constantly until mixture begins to thicken. Add butter 1 tbsp. at a time beating constantly until mixture is thick. I like to add fresh chopped tarragon to this sauce right before I serve it.

Kelli's Roasted Beet Salad

Bunch each of red and yellow (or orange beets)
Fresh Spring Greens Mix
Candied Walnuts
Goat, Bleu Cheese or Dublin Cheese chunks
3 Tbsp. Balsamic Vinegar
1 tsp sweet and sassy mustard
½ shallot minced
2 Tbsp. Extra Virgin Olive Oil

Roasting fresh beets will change anyone's opinion on beets if they don't love them already. Keep beets separated by color, peel and cut into 1 inch cubes. Place in shallow baking pan by color, cover bottom of pan equal amounts (¼ cup each) of port wine and red vinegar for red beets, and in separate pan, white wine and apple cider vinegar for yellow or orange beets. Cover with foil and roast at 400 for at least 30 minutes, beets should be caramelized. Let cool. Mix vinegar, mustard and shallots in small bowl, drizzle in olive oil to emulsify. Toss all ingredients in salad bowl. Cheese is personal preference.

Mary's Cream Puffs

Once Mary introduced these cream puffs to Girls' Night, they became a permanent fixture on the menu. First words on each year's menu planning—"Mary will bring the cream puffs." Period.

1 cup water

½ cup unsalted butter

1 tsp salt

1 cup all-purpose flour

4 eggs

In a large saucepan bring the water, butter and salt to a boil over medium heat. Add flour all at once and stir until a smooth ball forms. Remove from heat; let stand for 5 minutes. Add eggs one at a time, beating well after each addition. Continue beating until mixture is smooth and shiny. Scoop with melon scoop and drop onto greased baking sheet. Combine milk and egg yolk and brush over puffs. Bake at 400 degrees until golden brown, about 30-35 minutes. Remove to wire racks. Let cool completely.

Whip Cream:

1 pint Organic Valley Whipping Cream whipped to soft peak
(Put metal bowl and beaters in freezer before beating)

Add:

¼ cup sugar

1 tsp vanilla

Beat together on a lower speed to combine

Use very thin bladed serrated knife to cut a 2-3 inch horizontal slit in the puff and squeeze in the cream (use a plastic bag with corner cut off).

Kathleen's Breakfast Berry Bowl

@ The morning after involves four things…many pots of strong coffee, half & half, the oven pre-heated for assorted frozen quiches and a huge bowl of fresh berries. Kathleen always finds the most gorgeous, flavorful berries… strawberries, blackberries, raspberries, blueberries and then adds her secret ingredient: Chambord drizzled over all to add a hint of sweetness and to enhance the flavor.

Jeanne's Wine Cake (Shhh…don't tell Lydia!)

@ This is fabulous for dessert and delicious the next morning with coffee and berries.

1 Box Butter Recipe Cake Mix
1 small box instant vanilla pudding
½ cup vegetable oil
4 eggs
½ cup of dry white wine
½ cup of water

Topping:

1 cup sugar
½ cup dry white wine
½ cup of butter

Heat oven to 325 degrees. Butter and lightly flour Bundt cake pan, sprinkle with white sugar. Mix pudding mix, cake mix, wine, oil and eggs and beat for two minute. Pour batter into pan. Bake 55-60 minutes. Remove from oven, with skewer poke holes all over cake.

Acknowledgements

This book starts and ends with honoring Kathryn Goodwin and the life she created in her beloved Shelter at Pleasant Lake. I am grateful to carry on her spirit and traditions as time marches forward. To all the Pleasant Lake girls and the boys of Boyville, thank you for sharing precious lake time with me. And to sons Todd, Tom, Rob and Ben Goodwin, otherwise known as the Boneheads, I count myself lucky to make lake memories with you.

Thank you Miki Herman for once again affirming the journey of turning my notes into hard copy and to Jeff Larson, and Larson Design Company, for enthusiastically taking on the challenge of graphically fitting the puzzle pieces together to create the piece of art we now hold in our hands. We had fun all along the way and I will miss working with you on this project.

To my friends and family... ...thank you for listening to me repeatedly read out loud and especially to Kathy Russo, Jeanne Holbrook, Louise Sanborn, Judy Knowler and Lynn Wood, for your welcome suggestions and eagle eyes as we prepared to go to press. (It really does take a village to build a book.) And to my brother Thomas Russo, thank you for helping us across the finish line, I am eternally grateful for your support.

Finally, to my mostly companion and lake neighbor Matthew Goodwin...thank you for sharing Pleasant Lake with me all those years ago as we set off on our courtship. Little did I know how much that first paddle together would affect my future. I am ever thankful that we are growing old together at the Lake and still paddling on. To the next generations of Goodwin's at the lake… Todd, Tom, Rob, Ben, Sammy, Lucy, Leo, Holden (and those grandchildren yet to come), Cassie, Roscoe, Josh, Sadie and Natalie, this book is your legacy. We leave our lake traditions in your hands. You are the new spirit keepers of Pleasant Lake. Please hold her dear.

Anne and Matthew Goodwin